COLOR AT HOME

CREATING STYLE WITH PAINT

MEG AND STEVEN ROBERTS

THE ECHO DESIGN GROUP

Photographs by
ERIC LAIGNEL

Additional photography by
MEG AND STEVEN ROBERTS

Text by
BRENDA CULLERTON

STEWART, TABORI & CHANG | NEW YORK

Published in 2008 by Stewart, Tabori & Chang
An imprint of Harry N. Abrams, Inc.

Library of Congress Cataloging-in-Publication Data:

Roberts, Meg Lesser.
  Color at home : creating style with paint / Meg and
Roberts, Steven D.
    p. cm.
  ISBN 978-1-58479-663-3
  1. Color in interior decoration. 2. Color in architecture.
3. The Echo Design Group. I. Roberts, Steven D, 1956- II. Title.

NK2115.5.C6R62 2008
747'.94—dc22   2007026087

Editor: Kristen Latta
Designer: Susi Oberhelman
Production Manager: Jacquie Poirier

The text of this book was composed in Adrianna.

Printed and bound in China
10 9 8 7 6 5 4 3 2 1

HNA
harry n. abrams, inc.
a subsidiary of La Martinière Groupe

115 West 18th Street
New York, NY 10011
www.hnabooks.com

CONTENTS

Preface   8

Introduction   10

RED   14

ORANGE   32

YELLOW   46

GREEN   68

AQUA   94

BLUE   110

PURPLE   130

PINK   146

NEUTRALS   160

BLACK AND WHITE   182

Select Color Palettes   200

Credits   207

Acknowledgments   208

Color is in the air. At least it is at our company, The Echo Design Group. Since the company's inception in 1923, we have been designing scarves using print, pattern, and color to express our sense of what was beautiful and right for the time. The scarf, truly a versatile accessory, helped us hone our sensibilities and our understanding of how color can enhance a mood or an outfit or even provoke an emotional response.

From our roots in scarves, we have grown to design a myriad of fashion and home decorative products, from wallpaper and fabric to bedding and bath. In recent years, to celebrate our joy of home design, we published two books about the home. The first,

PREFACE

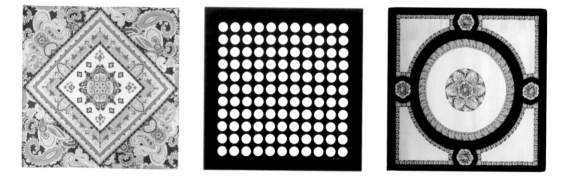

A Home for all Seasons (perhaps inspired by our fashion calendar), explored the seasonality of home décor. The second, *Time at Home*, was motivated by our own observation of the shrinking availability of this precious commodity and the need to celebrate it. We discovered that there is a relationship between the seasons and time, yet underlying it all is the influence of color.

Now to honor our 85th anniversary, we revisit the printed page to combine our long-standing love affair with color with our passion for the home. Color affects our mood, our dreams, our sense of self, and our environment. We can—and do—enrich our lives by exploring our interaction with our surroundings. To that end we have undertaken this project, an exploration of how color is used in the home, both interior and exterior. We don't profess to offer all solutions or a definitive how-to. This book simply shows examples of what we love.

Color is different inside and outside a home. Outside, color choice is greatly influenced by the locale, neighboring elements, architecture, and plantings. It was fascinating to explore how hues changed from morning to night, and season to season. Inside, many aspects of the room impacted our reaction to paint colors. The interplay of architecture, furniture, art, and natural light to the wall color offered wonderful contrasts and enhanced each others' strength and definition. We photographed city homes, as well as those in the country and suburbs. We found

no formula for right or wrong. Colors offer their own rhythms. Taste in color, as seems obvious, is extremely personal.

Colors have personalities. And like with people, those personalities can change depending on their surroundings or objects they come in contact with. We can develop relationships with colors. Some we will want nothing to do with; others we will form passionate relationships with. A special few will become family, with all their complexities, and will be with us for life.

Yes, color is in the air. It is all around us, all the time. It plays to our senses. It brightens our lives. It helps bring out our passions. There is nothing generic about color. It enriches our lives in ways we never realized. We love what color can do.

— MEG AND STEVEN ROBERTS

INTRODUCTION

Picasso had it right when he said: "You don't paint with colors. You paint with emotions." Few of us, of course, are gifted artists like Picasso. But think for a moment of common expressions: seeing red, feeling blue, tickled pink, green with envy. The connection between color and emotion is no coincidence. Color evokes intensely powerful feelings—feelings that are entirely personal. Subjective. When someone asks, "What's your favorite color?" the response is as spontaneous as it is instinctive, as passionate as it is primal. Color is a revelation of self; it can define who we are and how we feel.

There is something marvelous about this very personal and mysterious connection between color and our emotions. That color not only continues to move us so profoundly, to provoke, soothe, seduce, charm, and cajole but to also defy explanation, only makes that connection all the more precious and powerful.

We live with color everyday, and yet it can be intimidating. So why does the commitment to color, especially at home, demand an act of courage? Perhaps we're simply afraid of making mistakes. Perhaps we're hesitant to express our emotions in our surroundings because we're accustomed to being somewhat discreet with our feelings. In bringing them to the surface, we fear that we might reveal too much. Displaying emotion through the use of color in our homes does imply a degree of risk. But what is life without risk? (And keep in mind . . . Color is no more permanent than our moods. It is only permanent if we choose to make it so.)

Color, like beauty, is in the eye and the heart of the beholder. Whether you choose to use it sparingly or lavishly, whether you are attracted to the richest jewel-tones or the palest pastels, color is an exploration of energy and of pleasure, a private pleasure that captivates as it liberates. If you begin with a bold color choice in a mud room or bathroom, you may find it the perfect warm-up for taking risks in the living room or foyer. Think of an empty house as a blank canvas. What do you want to express? The peace of living in the moment? The longing for a new beginning? Even a childhood infatuation with the color red? Once you give yourself permission to be an artist, any fear is dissolved.

But where do you start? You might begin this exploration by asking yourself a few questions to help identify your own personal style and develop a vision for your home. "When and where am I the most comfortable?" "What makes me happy?" "What inspires me?" Questions play a pivotal role in every creative process. Envision the things and places you love. Close your eyes and imagine the burnished golds, faded pastels, and opulence of a vanished Venice or a sea as cool as pale jade. Think about the seasons you enjoy most. Envision a summer lawn as green as a maharajah's emeralds or the spectacular reds, oranges, and yellows of an autumn landscape. Spend an idle hour at the park or in a friend's garden, and dream of painting your room peony pink. Color is all around us. Color is a language, a language woven of memories, fantasy, impulse, and intuition. Think of it as an inner voice, a form of poetry or music that speaks without a need for words. Then listen to that voice. Open a dialogue. Free associate. Let the imagination loose.

The question of context is equally crucial in choosing the colors that both move you and fit within your own environment. Is your house in a city, near the ocean, or in the mountains? Do you dream of a space that reflects and absorbs that world outside, that is open to the elements and to a surfeit of sun and sky?

Or do you prefer an intimate, cozy space, the kind of deep-colored space that envelops the spirit and feels something like an embrace? Remember, too, that light has a dramatic impact on color and how it speaks to us.

Last but far from least, there is the question of architecture. Is your house modern? Colonial? Victorian? If so, you might consider a color palette that evokes those particular periods. You might also decide to abandon tradition and create a palette that is yours and yours alone. Ultimately, inspiration is a combination of all of these emotional links and leaps that make our lives unique.

Once you've located the colors that connect you to those emotional links, try them out. See how they feel. Sure, you might make mistakes. But that's the wonderful thing about paint. If it doesn't work, you paint over it. And when you actually get it right—when you open the Dutch red enamel door to a room painted lavender, the lavender so vibrant it seems to glow from within or walls washed in the palest, iridescent pink, a pink that shimmers like the inside of spiral seashell—it makes you feel almost giddy. The surprise of it. You grin like a child. That's the absolutely astonishing thing about color: the optimism, the fearlessness, the pure joy of it.

FIRE

RUBIES & RED

DESIRE

Red is the color of conquest. Of fearlessness, love, and seduction. Like stop signs and brake lights, red grabs your attention. Even tiny hummingbirds prefer to hover over red flowers. As strong as red is, it is a primary color and therefore is appealing to both men and women, young and old. It is as American as apple pie. But like an irresistible impulse, it can also lead the imagination to faraway places such as India, China, and Turkey. Red with black and white, whether in the

A FIERCE INTENSITY OF BEING

shape of a piano or a series of framed black and white portraits, is elegant and timeless. For a blaze of excitement, try a tomato red with other strong colors—yellow, green, violet, or blue. High-gloss lacquer reds have an exotic Asian quality. Barn reds, hennas, and crimson bring a touch of fall and earthiness. Like savoring a sip of vintage Bordeaux, stepping into a den painted in warm wine or maroon, s a perfect end to a day. Red is a color that generates power and passion; it won't be overlooked. Delightfully defiant, it is well worth the risk.

LOVE AT FIRST SIGHT

REFRESHING AS TROPICAL PUNCH

THE COLOR OF SEDUCTION

RADIANT

SULTRY ORANGE

SIZZLE

There's endless possibility in the juicy allure of orange. Like the fruit it is named after, orange is refreshing and bold. Bright, sun-kissed orange is not for the faint of heart. But it can be a genuine delight, open and gregarious. Between yellow and red, orange takes the best qualities from each parent, mixing the dynamic heat of red with the carefree optimism of yellow. The more red and rosy the orange, the more comfortable it becomes; the more yellow and acidic, the more adventurous. Salmon has a softer, less edgy feel than

INTOXICATING JOY OF AUTUMN

a citrus, kumquat orange. When used full force, orange can be tamed by white trim or rich leathers. Move towards peach and create a honeyed glow in any room. Peach can be sweet but mixed with dark, stained wood, it becomes worldly. Dip into the glorious colors of autumn—browns, rusts, and clay—and the color orange becomes earthy, organic. Modern design is infatuated with orange; when combined with brown it is the height of fashion chic. From pumpkin to pomegranate, amber to apricot, tangerine to terra cotta, the moods of orange are as infinitely varied as our own.

AS VITAL AND GLOWING AS HOPE

A SHOCKING WASH OF **LIGHT**

THE WARMTH OF A SMOLDERING FIRE

SPRING'S SWEET YELLOW SHOUT

ike a rain slicker on a stormy day, yellow brightens even the smallest, darkest room. Just think for a moment of an armful of spring forsythia. Or a field of daffodils. Brave, even playful, yellow is also enormously versatile and popular. From the palest French vanilla to the deepest gold, it radiates a magical, cheerful light. A swath of sunshine yellow, stretched like a canvas and studded with white polka dots, looks like a piece of modern art in an urban

A CERTAIN CLARITY OF LIGHT

loft. Maize clapboard, inside and out, is as friendly as it is familiar. Dark shutters deliver a crisp sense of dignity to a yellow exterior, while a touch of green mutes the effect and blends in beautifully with natural surroundings. Only when yellow leans toward green does it require a bit more audacity. Deep yellow ochre and antique golds cast a lush, aged beauty to any room. There is something extravagant about the color yellow, about the way it illuminates a space and brings such warmth and daylight into our lives.

THE COLOR OF SWEET BUTTER

THE BEGINNING OF A **NEW DAY**

THE SLOW **DRIP** OF **HONEY**

LUCK
ENVY &
EMERALDS

GREEN

Green means life. From a field of spring grass to the leaves of the mightiest oak, green is the most vital color in nature. As shady, quieting parks of a city offer escape, the perfect green room can offer sanctuary, a retreat. Simultaneously soothing and invigorating, green can do no less than restore your spirit. It may have more varied hues, values, and characters than any other color, some of which are the most comfortable, usable, and timeless tones in home design. Celadon, avocado, olive, forest, hunter:

PERFUME OF PINE AND MINT

there has hardly been a time in history when one of these greens wasn't popular. Sage is so familiar and user-friendly, it has become nearly neutral. But today, lime, kelly green, and cool mints are decorator favorites. Greens mixed with neutrals or other greens become casual, natural. The cleaner, brighter, or more yellow the green, the bolder it becomes; the darker or bluer, the more traditional and masculine. However you use it, there is a shade of green to enhance any style. Whether it's *the* environment or a more personal home environment, the whole world is going green.

A MAGICAL **FAIRY-TALE** FOREST

THE AROMA OF **FRESHLY MOWN GRASS**

A PEACE OF GREEN

JUBILANT
GENTLE   AQUA
SPLASH

Aqua is a divine cocktail. Color with a spirited kick. It can be as seductive as the sounds of salsa yet remarkably soft and gentle. Bleached to the color of sea glass, it conjures up visions of honeymoons and slow-motion swimming in jewel-like seas. Equally at home in a nursery as in a formal living room, aqua leads a double life. For a tropical feel, mix it with fresh oranges, yellows, and

THE LURE OF A TAHITIAN LAGOON

fuchsias. Add a bit of black and white or sterling silver and it's the essence of designer glamour. Deepen it to rich turquoise, peacock, or petrol and the color is more complex and unusual than its blue and green cousins. Aqua can create a room from an otherwise insignificant nook or kick a kitchen cupboard up a notch. Aqua stands up to the boldest furnishings and most eclectic artwork. Exhilarating and unexpected, a life lived in aqua is like bringing a Caribbean vacation, home.

THE SHIMMER OF SWIMMING POOLS

LIVING THE LIFE AQUATIC

THE COOLNESS OF MORNING MIST

Born of an almost everlasting sense of cool, blue is an inspired choice. Baby blue or navy, Tiffany blue or Wedgewood, blue retains its classic identity in all its tones. Royal blue is strong and bright while clear periwinkle is bold, vibrant but friendly. Serenely self-assured, blue creates a spa-like aura in bathrooms. It can also induce a sense of well-being and welcome sleepiness in the bedroom. Robin's egg blue feels expensive, especially with

A LONG, SLOW TRUMPET SOLO

accents of chocolate brown and black. As ubiquitous as blue interiors are, the color is always a surprise. Inviting and embracing, it seems to welcome guests to your home. Outdoors, blue is in its element. Blue exteriors with white trim are fresh, cheerful. Black trims seem stately, distinguished. Perhaps because of our profound connection to the water and sky, blue is a natural. Stepping into a blue room is as cozy and familiar as slipping on your favorite pair of jeans.

THE MYSTERIOUS **PULL OF THE DEEP**

A WIDE-OPEN EXPANSE OF SUMMER SKY

THE **HEART** OF A **HOT** FLAME

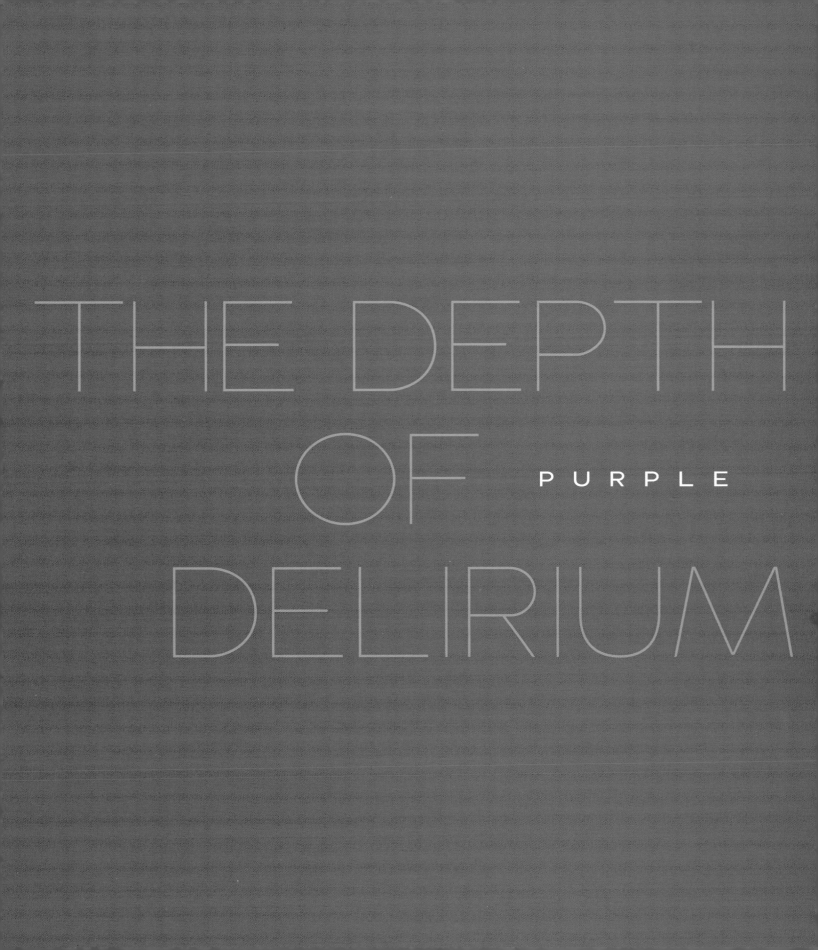

THE DEPTH OF DELIRIUM

PURPLE

From the palest lavender to the deepest black plum, purple is a revelation—creative, artistic. Purple is a bit more eccentric and complex than its closest relatives, fuchsia and indigo. Throughout history, purple has been associated with royalty; today, purple in the home is still rare and refined. Even if taking the plunge into purple demands a bit of bravery, the color creates a fabulous first—and lasting—impression. Deep violets and plums work

HEATHER SHROUDED IN MIST

the same wonders for precious textiles, artwork, and the polished patina of antiques as they do for the stark drama of modern furnishings. Not strictly for grown-ups, purple in a young girl's room feels special, unique. Delicate lilac paired with white lace is quaint, nostalgic. Purple shutters, from grape to eggplant, are a delightful surprise, as is the jolt of a rich, Prince-purple formal living room. Purple is always unexpected but undeniably welcome. Vivid and full of character, purple reigns.

THE FRAGRANCE OF WISTERIA AND LILAC

A PLAY ON THE COLOR PURPLE

ICING

BALLET   PINK

LIPSTICK

No longer just for little girls, people now "think pink" everywhere from country farmhouses to maxed-out modern lofts. You might say pink has a split personality. Yes, it can be soft and reassuring, but it can also be sexy and hot. Pink can be bright bubblegum, deep raspberry, or muted antique mauve. It can be predictable, as in a girl's nursery, or boldly unexpected when seen in darker shades in a stately living room. Few colors are as traditional in the

THE COLOR OF ANTICIPATION

home as rose—from tea rose to dusty rose to rosewood. But these days, pink has given way to shades with far more flamboyant personalities. Think of the pop of a cotton candy–colored Victorian house in a New England snowstorm or the sophistication of flamingo-pink walls in a dining room. Take bright lipstick pink, accent it with black and gold, and the look is couture sleek. Pure chic. Young in spirit, neon pink and fuchsia are frisky, flirtatious. In short, pink is demure...and daring, full of all the joyful contradictions of everyday life.

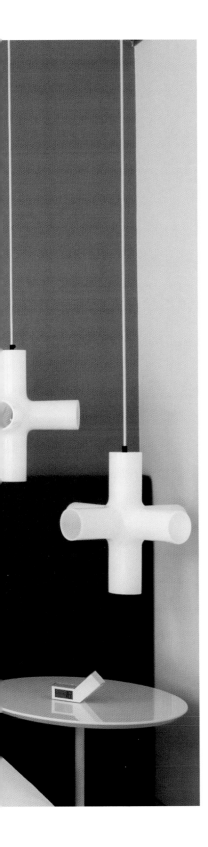

THE GIDDY EXTRAVAGANCE OF YOUTH

155

SMOOTH, SILKY SKIN OF **SEASHELLS**

MOMENTS
IN
NEUTRAL
PAUSE

A true artist sees color where others see neutrals. Put a variety of neutrals together and suddenly pinks, greens, oranges, and golds emerge as anything but bland and uninspired. In fact, there is a subtle richness and texture to a well-designed neutral palette. Colors from ivory and beige, through khaki and mushroom, to sepia and espresso can be used to wonderful effect. Don't confuse ivory, bone, or vanilla for simple white, as these colors—while basic—bring warmth and softness to any room or

TOES SNUGGLING IN HOT SAND

exterior. Middle shades of cocoa, suede, and taupe are a far cry from a "sea of beige." And deep shades of coffee bean and fudge transform any den or living room into a stylishly dramatic space. For those who find bright, jarring colors difficult to live with, neutrals offer a comfortable alternative. Try using bright orange accessories and flowers to add the perfect kick to a rich brown living room or a delightful red door on a grey and black house. In short, think fashion; think cashmere, mink, or pearl. All neutral. All rich. All timeless.

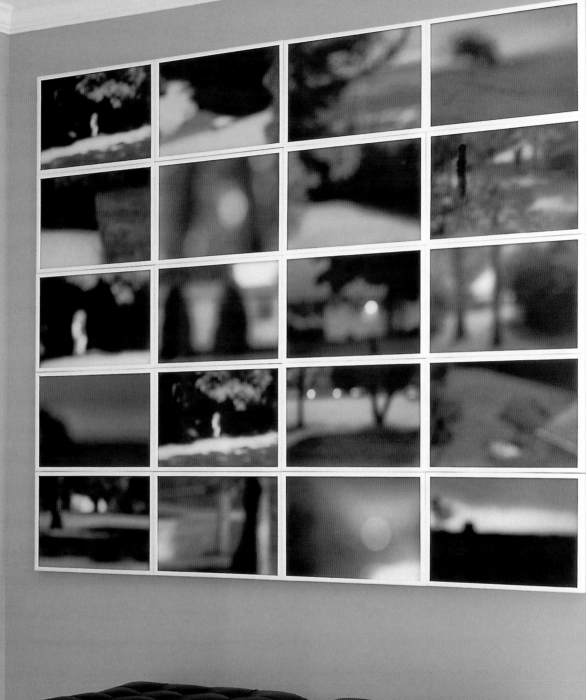

THE **CLEAN LINES** OF AN ARTIST'S **SKETCH**

THE CRACKLING OF BIRCH BARK

THE TASTE OF **BITTERSWEET CHOCOLATE**

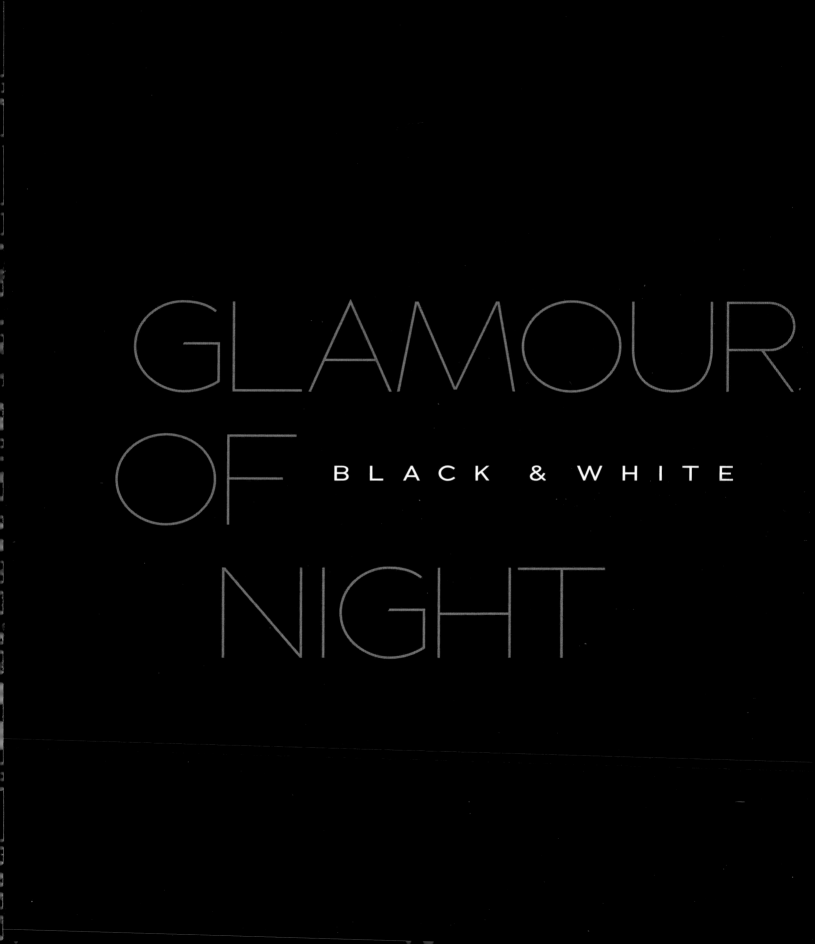

GLAMOUR
OF
NIGHT

BLACK & WHITE

There is no simpler way to make a dramatic statement than to limit your color palette to black and white. Clean, bold, urban, and chic, the two together are truly timeless. Forever current. White alone is a blank canvas. In fact, the majority of walls in America are painted white. But an all-white room also shows strength of character, assuredness, restraint, and discipline. Black, of course, is even more daring and should be used with finesse so as not to appear too dark or somber. As retro as it is modern, black is

AN EXAGGERATED POINT OF VIEW

about glamour and style. And then there are all the shades of grey. Mix grey with metallics and the look is urban industrial. Combined with the warmth of wood and natural materials, grey becomes marvelously comfortable, soothing. Deep charcoal, never as severe as black, is both rich and enveloping. A clapboard home, painted grey or pewter, with white mullions and black shutters, is eternally elegant. Add a bright red door or plant a flowering tree or vividly colored tulips and it's like accessorizing your favorite suit.

NIGHTS IN WHITE SATIN

A HANDFUL OF LOOSE **PEARLS**

PALETTES

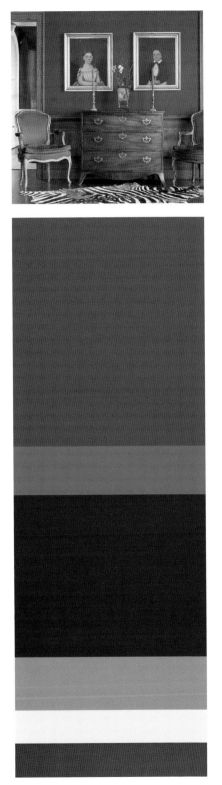

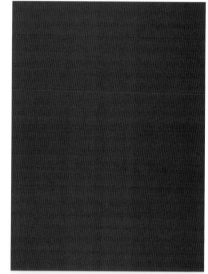

CREDITS

We are very grateful to all the people listed below who so generously opened their doors and shared their homes with us. Their passions and creativity were contagious.

Susan and Mark Alcott
Janet and Steve Bear
Patricia Beeck
Casey and Chuck Berg
Alice and Norman Bloom
Elizabeth and Forrest Butler
Diane Duncan Cady
Amy and Jay M. Courage
Kristin Clotilde Darnell
Michelle and Fred Daum
Nicol Butters and Trip Davis
Jeffrey Einhorn
Laura G. Farrell
Sandi and John Fifield
Bob and Roberta Fisher
Fraerman Associates Architecture
Jeff and Lisa Friedstein
Amy and George Goldstein
Michele and William Gorski
Timothy and Deanna Gould
Flora Lazar and Lee Greenhouse
Leslie and Dan Gregg
Cricket and Rob Guyton
Molly Hardie
Evan and Michelle Hughes
Lara and Tony Ignaczak
Abbie Jordan
Molly B. Lazar

Jessica Tampas and Richard Lazar
Suzy, John, and Eleanor LeBoutillier
James H. and Constance A. Levi
Sally Lou and Mitchell Loveman
Lucy Buckley Maloney
Josh and Ravit Mandell
Sharon Manering
Meegan McMillan
Carolyn and Jim Millstein
Beth and Kevin Mullaney
Tom and Lisa Nelson
Tom and Claire O'Connor
Jim and Jane Orthwein
Frances Palmer
James Pendry
Fred and Retha Petrosino
Judith and Harvey Rubin
Amy Frolick and Brad Scheler
Jane and Joel Schneider
Lisa O. Schultz
Linda and Ben Seltzer
Joyce and Jim Seymore
Kia Shea Silverman
Melina Vourlekis
Debbie and Richard Ward
The Waters Family
Jamie Zimmerman

Interior Design: Patricia Beeck: 26, 32, 88, 89; Amy and Jay M. Courage: 81, 94, 101; Brian del Toro of Bunny Williams, Inc.: 30, 31, 78, 82; Jeanne-Aelia Desparmet-Hart: 20; Jeffrey B. Einhorn of the St. James Design Group, LLC: 6; Robin Ellis: 106, 188; Jocie Fifield: 154-55; Amy Frolick: 12, 41, 75, 80, 85, 99; Barclay FRYERY: 77, 141, 193, 197; Steven Gambrel of SR Gambrel, Inc: 129, 149; Leslie Gregg: 91, 125, 187; Molly Hardie: 68, 137, 170; Lisa Lipschutz-Abode: 156; Lucy Buckley Maloney: 62; Greg McKenzie of Duhallow Interiors: 185; Meegan McMillan of Alcara Design, Inc: 12, 14, 17, 117, 134, 139, 172; Frances and Wallace Palmer: 178-79; Judy Pollard of Cottage Interiors: 72-73, 108, 109, 121, 128, 166, 176; Schema Interiors: 2, 102, 181

Art: Eric Aho: 169; Jocie Fifield: 154-55; Sandi Haber Fifield: 163; Stuart Frolick: 41; Jessica Tampas Photography: 181; Amanda Means: 18; Carolyn Millstein: 126; Frances Palmer: 178-79; Zoey B. Scheler: 75, 80, 99; Joyce Seymore: 24, 174, 190; Ion Zupcu: 19

Architecture: Fraerman Associates Architecture: 136, 140; Jay Smith: 174, 190

Photography: All photographs by Eric Laignel except the following: Amy L. Courage: 100; Meg and Steven Roberts: 1, 5, 12, 13, 37, 38, 42-43, 44, 54, 55, 58, 61, 62, 84, 86, 93, 104, 118, 119, 123, 142, 144-45, 151, 152, 157, 159, 175, 177, 186, 189, 192; William Waldron at Achard Associates: 149

Please visit Echo's website at www.echodesign.com.

ACKNOWLEDGMENTS

We always consider a book project a wonderful adventure. Meeting and working with new and old friends is one of the great rewards. Thankfully there is a strong and supportive internal team at Echo. We would like to thank Dorothy and Lynn Roberts (Steven's mother and sister) who work alongside us every day and give us the freedom to pursue this passion. Diane Baker, Echo's Director of Licensing, contributed in every way possible. Without her this book might not exist. Michelle Krautheim and Susan Azizo, who make up the core of our home design team, kept all else moving in such positive ways.

We were so excited to have assembled such a strong book team. Eric Laignel, our expert photographer, embraced this project with great enthusiasm, a necessary sense of adventure, and a wonderful spirit. Our graphic designer, Susi Oberhelman, took a huge stack of photographs, the text, and a lot of varied input and brought the book to life in a clean and imaginative way. Brenda Cullerton, our repeat writer and resident thinker, added the poetry to help the book flow.

All throughout we were blessed with the consistent, gentle focus of Kristen Latta, our editor. We thank her and the entire team at Stewart, Tabori & Chang and Abrams who have been so supportive throughout our relationship, which now spans more than ten years.

Looking for locations is never easy. Yet the process moves much more successfully with talented, tasteful people running in advance. We want to thank Elaine Stimmel, Lou Pollak, Jeanne-Aelia Desparmet-Hart, and Sandi Haber Fifield for scouting so many interesting homes. Amy Courage (Meg's sister, who is a talented architect in her own right), Jane Schneider, and Loree Sandler deserve a big thank-you, not only for finding locations but also assisting with the styling.

We also thank our home product partners who have supported us and the Echo brand for years by bringing world-class quality product to market. They are Revman International, Creative Bath Products, Kravet Fabrics, CR Gibson, Elrene Home Fashions, Kensington Home Fashions, and Brewster Wallcoverings.

For many years, stopping along the road and photographing homes has been a passion. So we wish to thank the homeowners we don't even know for inspiring this book at its outset. You now know who you are.

Finally, as always, we want to thank Sam, Charlie, Lily, Barbara, and Toby, who provide so much color at home.